Nelson

Handwriting

Developing Skills

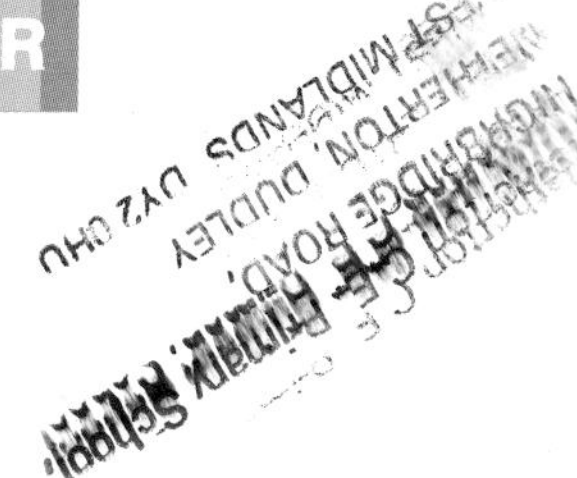

Anita Warwick
Series editor: John Jackman

CONTENTS/SCOPE AND SEQUENCE

Page	Focus	Extra	Extension	Focus resource	Extension resource
4-5 Flashback	*Flashback*	*Flashback*	*Flashback*	*Flashback*	*Flashback*
6-7 Unit 1 Wartime	revising sloped writing	choose words using the prefixes aero, trans and micro and copy sentences	copy passage about codes, using fluent and legible handwriting	practise making patterns and letters with a slope, copy words with a prefix	revise sloped letters
8-9 Unit 2 Wartime	ensuring letters are the correct height and size	choose words using the prefix counter and copy sentences	copy passage, ensuring letters are the correct height and size	practise making patterns and letters the correct height and size	copy poem, ensuring letters are correct height and size
10-11 Unit 3 Shipwrecks	practising spacing	practise writing speech marks	use notes to write a short biography, remembering to leave a space between letters	copy words containing unstressed vowels, join letters correctly to ensure correct spacing	write out sentences, adding speech marks and leaving a correct space between letters and words
12-13 Unit 4 Shipwrecks	practising speedwriting	finish writing notes	copy reporter's finished article	underline main points in article and write the notes from which it was written	copy passage quickly but neatly
14-15 Unit 5 Victorians	practising drafting and editing	copy and edit the first draft of newspaper article	write final draft of newspaper article	correct the spelling mistakes and write a paragraph about Brunel in best handwriting	edit first draft of a short biography about Darwin, copy corrected final draft in best handwriting
16-17 Unit 6 Victorians	practising writing capital letters	copy sentences and insert the missing capital letters	copy passage from Mary Seacole's autobiography	copy poem	copy extract and insert the missing capital letters
18-19 Unit 7 Mysteries and the unexplained	practising fluency	copy sentences and insert a descriptive word from Focus section	copy passage, using quick, fluent and legible handwriting	choose a verb to complete each sentence, change the ending to ed or ing, copy sentences	practise writing fluently and legibly, copy poem
20-21 Unit 8 Mysteries and the unexplained	practising paragraphs	write information as two paragraphs	write an account of a Yeti hunt as three paragraphs	copy paragraph about the Sphinx in best handwriting	divide passage about Standing Stones into two paragraphs, copy them in best handwriting
22-23 Unit 9 Aliens	practising keeping letters in the correct proportion	choose the correct word, either with prefix un or not, and copy passage	copy poem	copy sentences, inserting correct word containing prefix dis	copy poem
24-25 Unit 10 Aliens	practising presentation	copy text for birthday party invitation	design and make an invitation to an Aliens Fancy Dress Party	copy/design a certificate for winning fancy dress competition	Write and present a thank-you letter, write a reply to letter

Page	Focus	Extra	Extension	Focus resource	Extension resource
26-27 Unit 11 Safety first	practising writing instructions	copy sentences and insert the correct connective word	put instructions from The Green Cross Code in correct order and copy them	use connectives to join sentences about firework safety	follow instructions for designing a poster about a fireworks display
28-29 Unit 12 Safety first	practising writing instructions	copy instructions for cyclists turning right at a road junction	design and make a leaflet about buying and maintaining a bicycle	put instructions for making a pizza in the correct order and copy	design a poster about wearing seat belts
30-31 Unit 13 Ancient Greece	practising presenting a project (handwriting for different purposes)	read and make notes on passage about the origin of the Olympic Games	use best handwriting to write a passage about the Olympic Games then and now from notes	put the rocket launches that led up to the first Moon landing in the correct order on a chart	copy poem about how it might feel to land on the Moon in best handwriting
32-33 Unit 14 Ancient Greece	practising fluency	copy passage, inserting the pronouns he or him to make it easier to read	copy extract about Narcissus in fluent, joined and legible writing	use fluent handwriting to copy passage about the Ancient Greeks	use fluent handwriting to copy passage about Medusa, underline pronouns
34-35 Unit 15 Cliffs and treasure	practising writing double letters	choose correct word and copy sentences	copy passage containing words with double letters	choose synonyms, copying double letters within words carefully	copy poem, underline words with double letters
36-37 Unit 16 Cliffs and treasure	practising speedwriting	write out notes in full, using neat handwriting	copy sentences quickly, using abbreviations as necessary	copy two sentences quickly but legibly to find writing speed	copy quickly a list of 20 words to do with treasure
38-39 Unit 17 Cats	ensuring letters are in the correct proportion	choose the correct word to complete each simile	think of a simile to finish sentences, copy sentences with letters the correct shape, size and height	choose a word to complete each simile	copy similes, ensuring letters are in correct proportion, and match sentences with similes
40-41 Unit 18 Cats	practising presentation	copy list of kennings about a cat, thinking carefully about presentation	write own kennings poem and illustrate it	put acrostic poem about cats in correct order, copy it and make it attractive	copy poem and illustrate it
42-43 Unit 19 Travellers' tales	practising printing	copy advert, using the print alphabet	copy poster, using the print alphabet	use print letters to copy fact sheet about a theme park	copy chart showing prices of two-day breaks at different hotels
44-45 Unit 20 Travellers' tales	developing an individual handwriting style	copy sentences in different styles of writing	copy extract, using own preferred style of writing	copy poem, making joins after the letters b and p and loops from f, g and j	copy lines, making joins after b and p and loops from f, g and y
46-48 Check-up	*Check-up*	*Check-up*	*Check-up*	*Check-up*	*Check-up*

OCUS

A Copy these patterns into your book.

amamam wewewewe

B Copy these words into your book. Make sure all your letters are the correct height and size.

twenty forty Monday Wednesday
family familiar heavy heavily

C Copy these words into your book. Make sure your writing is sloped slightly to the right.

faithfully sincerely fitter fittest
light heavy join constellation

XTRA

Copy these words into your book using fluent and legible handwriting.
Check you are making the joins correctly.

mine my yes no his new
near he her plane plain

dull night theatre boats
shop shopping nation

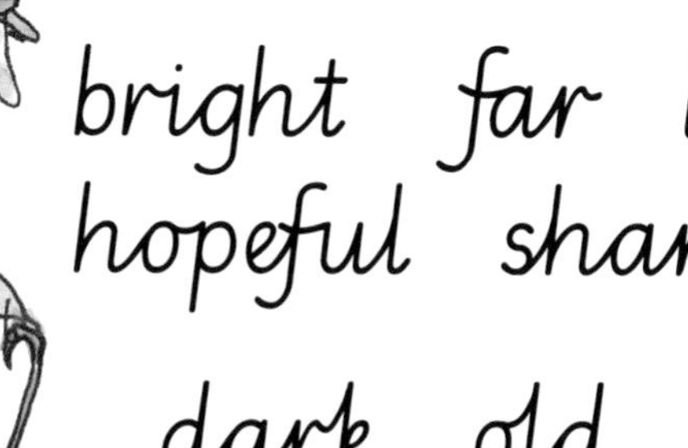

bright far long knives
hopeful share sharing

dark old short fearful
flew flue who's whose

telephone relaxed lizard
joyful bright flying queen

XTENSION

Copy this poem into your book.

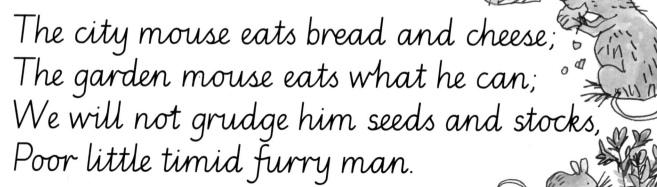

The city mouse eats bread and cheese;
The garden mouse eats what he can;
We will not grudge him seeds and stocks,
Poor little timid furry man.

From **'The City Mouse and the Garden Mouse'** by *Christina Rossetti*

UNIT 1

Revising sloped writing.

Cryptographers solve ciphers.

FOCUS

Copy these words into your book. Remember to slope your writing slightly to the right.

aeroplane transplant microdot
aerobatics transport microscope
aerodrome transaction microscopic

Remember to turn your paper at a slight angle and pull the pen strokes in the correct direction.

XTRA

Copy these sentences into your book. Choose the correct word. Use a dictionary to check the meaning of any unfamiliar words.

1 Many women learned to fly aeroplanes/aerodromes during the Second World War.

2 Aeroplanes were used to transport/transaction troops and drop agents behind enemy lines.

3 A microdot/microscope is a tiny photograph of a coded message.

When sloping your handwriting, remember that all your letters must have the same slope.

XTENSION

Copy this passage into your book. Remember to write fluently and legibly.

A code replaces the words of a message with letters, numbers or symbols. A cipher adds or substitutes letters or numbers to disguise the message. Codes and ciphers were used a lot in the Second World War. Cryptographers found out valuable information by deciphering messages sent from cipher machines.

UNIT 2

Ensuring letters are the correct height and size.

The defence was too strong for the attacking force.

FOCUS

Copy these words into your book. Make sure all your letters are the correct height and size.

counteract counterbalance counterfeit
countermove counterweight counterfoil
counterpoise countermeasure countermand

Be careful, these letters should all be the same height:
a c e i m n o r s u v w x z

XTRA

Copy these sentences into your book. Use a dictionary to help you choose the correct word.

1 The captain was cross because he had been paid in counterbalance/counterfeit money.

2 The village planned to counteract/counterfoil the invasion of the army.

3 The fort was filled with soldiers as a countermeasure/counterpoise.

XTENSION

Copy this passage into your book. Remember to make your letters the correct height and size.

Remember, the descender, or tail, on these letters falls below the line:

f g j p q y

Instead of hillforts, the Iron Age people in Scotland and Wales built small circular stone forts for defence. In the north of Scotland and the islands, chiefs defended their homes with tall circular towers. These are called brochs and many can still be seen. The best example is on Mousa Island in the Shetland Isles.

From ***'Places of Defence'*** by *Gillian Clegg*

UNIT 3

Practising spacing.

"Can I row with you?" Grace Darling pleaded.

A Copy these words into your book.

frightened shouted pleaded
lighthouse determined although

B Copy this sentence into your book.

Although Grace was frightened, she pleaded with her father to let her row with him to rescue the survivors of the shipwreck.

Remember, leaving an equal space between your letters and an equal space between your words will help make your handwriting easy to read.

EXTRA

A conversation can be written down exactly as it is spoken, by using speech marks. A comma is added before the last speech mark, like this:

"I can see people on the rocks and in the water," shouted Grace.

Remember, speech marks are written at the same height as ascenders.

Copy these sentences into your book. Leave an equal space between your letters and an equal space between your words. Add the missing speech marks and commas.

1 We can't just leave them to drown sobbed Grace.

2 Grace, the sea is very rough said her father.

3 If we both go, we can row together pleaded Grace.

EXTENSION

When someone else writes information about the life of a real person, it is called a biography. Use the notes below to make a short biography of Grace Darling. Write it into your book in your best handwriting.

Remember, letters must not touch each other, like this:

er × er ✓

Grace Darling (1815-42)

Her father was a lighthouse keeper.

In 1838, a boat called the 'Forfarshire' struck rocks near the lighthouse.

Grace and her father rowed out in a small boat to rescue the survivors.

They had to make their trip through huge waves.

They became famous for their great bravery.

UNIT 4

Practising speedwriting.

10.00 arr. to see shp sinkg. Lot of oil.

FOCUS

Copy these notes and their meaning into your book. Write out what the last four notes mean.

Notes	**Meaning**
10/8/1628 shp 'Vasa' lauchd	On the 10th August 1628, the ship 'Vasa' is launched.
shp lves stckhlm hrbr	The ship leaves Stockholm harbour.
Sud'nly gst wnd blws shp ovr	
shp snks in 33m wtr	
trav'l'd jst 1,300m	

XTRA

Reporters have to write quickly to record what they see. Copy this table into your book. Finish the notes made by the reporter in speedwriting.

What the reporter saw	The notes the reporter made
It is January 1993. Off the coast of the Shetland Islands, an oil tanker called 'Braer' is adrift.	Jan 93 oil tnkr

XTENSION

This is the article the reporter wrote later from his notes. Copy it into your book.

Remember, sloping your writing slightly to the right helps you to write quickly.

It was a cold January day in 1993. I reached the clifftop at about 10 am. Below me I could see the 'Braer' drifting towards the rocky coast of the Shetland Islands. Waves pounded the ship. The tugboats couldn't get close.

Suddenly the ship struck rocks. I saw oil spread slowly across the sea. As the tanker began to sink, a helicopter arrived and winched the crew to safety.

UNIT 5

Practising drafting and editing.

Drafting your writing helps you get it right.

The three stages of drafting, editing and final copy are below. Look at them and write the final copy into your book.

When writing a first draft, you do not need to use your best handwriting as no one else is going to read it.

Isimbard Kingdom Brunell was 1 of Britains gretest engnears.

Is~~i~~[a]mbard Kingdom Brunel~~l~~
was ~~1~~[one] of Britain's gr~~e~~[a]test
engine~~a~~[e]rs.

Isambard Kingdom Brunel
was one of Britain's
greatest engineers.

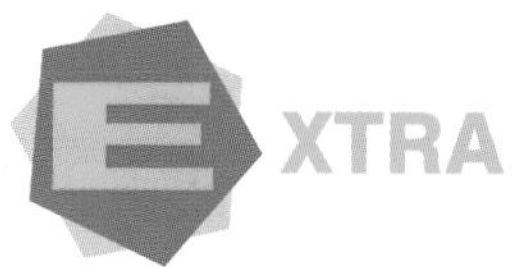

Read this draft. Some of the draft has been edited. Copy the draft into your book and correct the rest of the mistakes.

Is~~i~~a mbard Kingdom Brunel~~l~~ was

1 of Britains gretest enginears.

1826 he began working on the

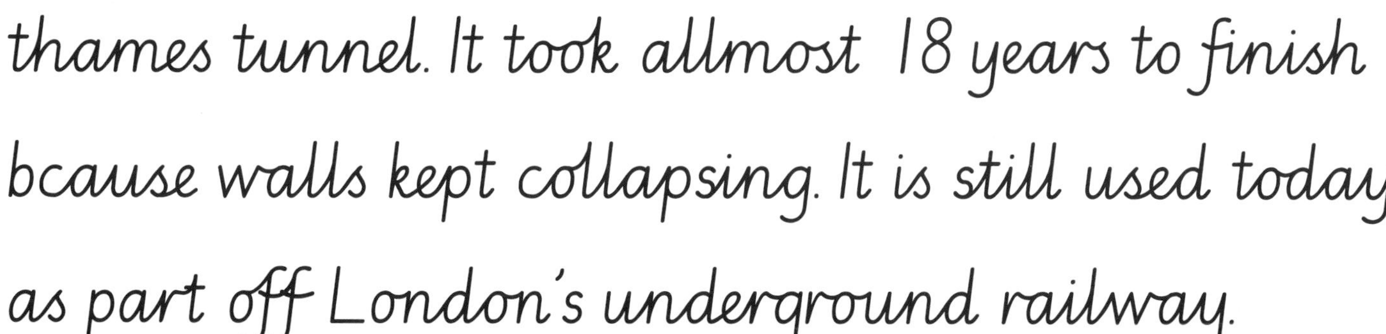

thames tunnel. It took allmost 18 years to finish

bcause walls kept collapsing. It is still used today

as part off London's underground railway.

This tribute to Isambard Kingdom Brunel has been drafted and edited. Write the final copy into your book.

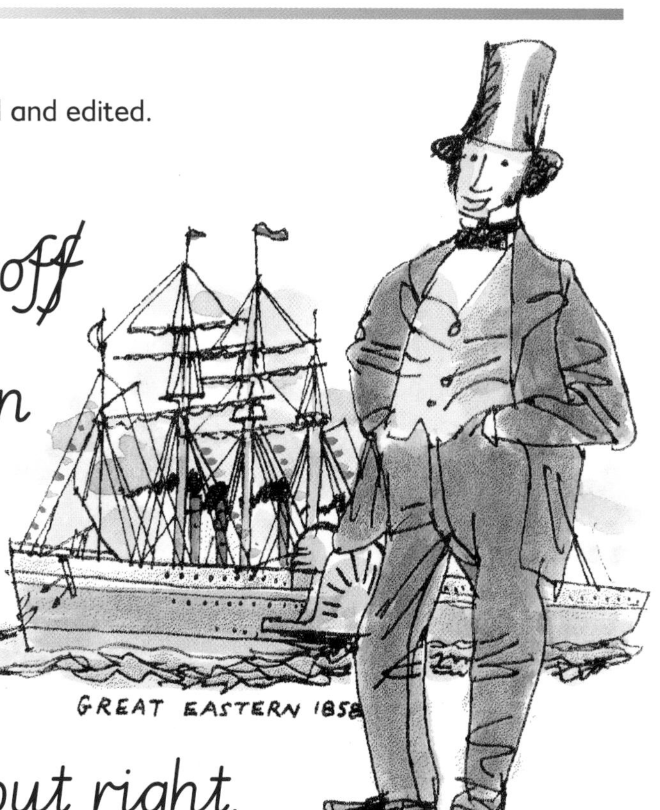

By his de~~f~~ath the great~~i~~est of~~f~~

Britain's eng~~e~~ineers ha~~d~~s been

lost. ~~He~~ Brunel was a man with

striking originality of

thou~~f~~ght, bold in ~~her~~ his plans but right.

UNIT 6

Practising writing capital letters.

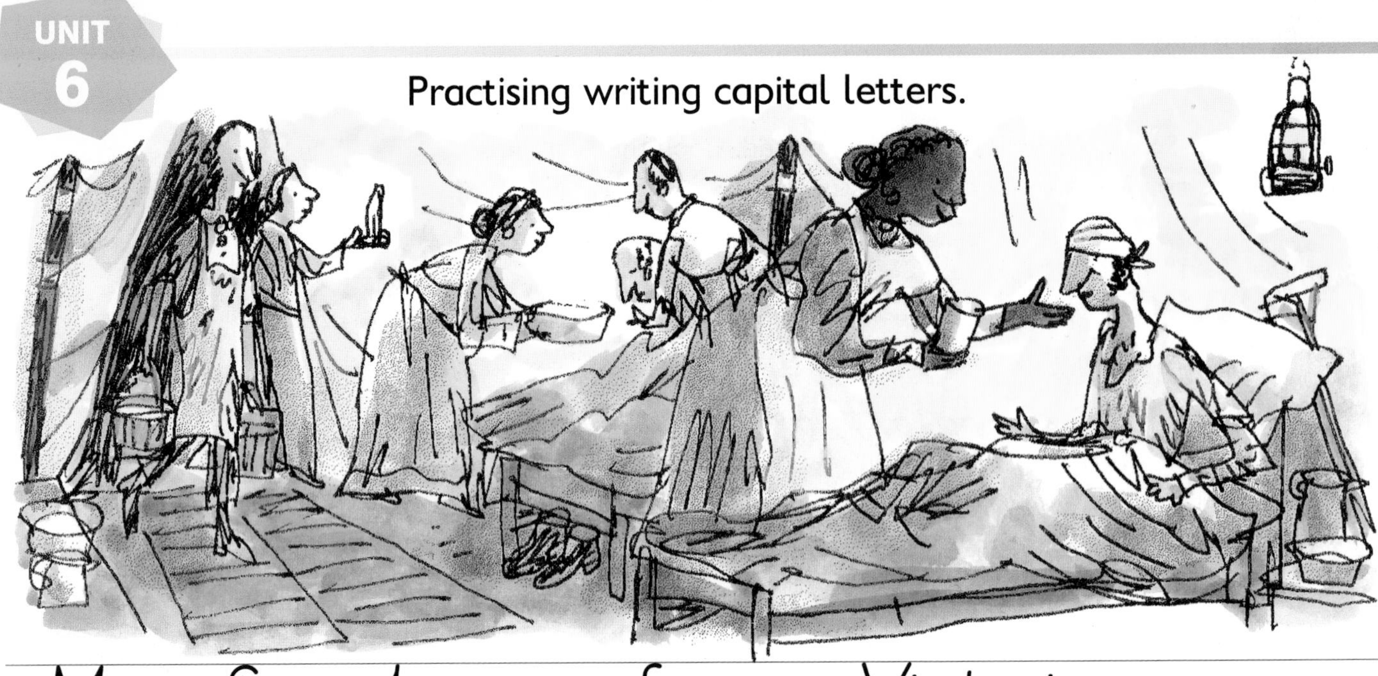

Mary Seacole was a famous Victorian.

FOCUS

Here is each capital letter with its lower-case version. Copy the letters three times into your book.

Aa Bb Cc Dd Ee Ff Gg Hh Ii Jj
Kk Ll Mm Nn Oo Pp Qq Rr Ss
Tt Uu Vv Ww Xx Yy Zz

XTRA

These sentences show what Mary Seacole did. Copy them into your book.
Add the missing capital letters. The first one is done to help you.

Remember,
capital letters are the same height as ascenders.

I knew the hospitals in the Crimea were filthy and rat-infested.

1 i volunteered my services to the army, but i was rejected.

2 so i travelled to the crimea and opened the british hotel.

3 wherever i went i took medicines and food for the soldiers.

XTENSION

This is an extract from Mary Seacole's account of her own life, her autobiography.
Copy the extract into your book. Make sure your capital letters are as tall as ascenders.

The first day that I approached the wharf (at Balaclava) a party of sick and wounded had just arrived. Seeing a poor artilleryman I ran up to him at once, and eased the stiff dressing and well was I rewarded when the poor fellow's groans subsided into a restless easy mutter.

From ***'Wonderful Adventures of Mrs Seacole in Many Lands'***

Remember,
capital letters are break letters.

UNIT 7

Practising fluency.

Fluent writing flows quickly!

FOCUS

Copy these words into your book. Remember to join your letters.

stare	whine	crackle	whistle
stared	whined	crackled	whistled
staring	whining	crackling	whistling

Sloping your writing and forming your joins correctly will help make your handwriting fluent.

XTRA

Use a word from the **Focus** on page 18 to finish these sentences. Copy the sentences into your book. Remember to write fluently and legibly.

1 The wind ________ through the trees.

2 I could hear a dog ________ in the distance.

3 Suddenly I heard the log fire ________.

4 Then I saw two eyes ________ at me.

XTENSION

Copy this passage into your book, using fluent handwriting.

There were strange whining noises and odd whistling sounds that Imran couldn't identify. He felt a shiver run down his spine. What could the noises be? He crept forward. Suddenly he heard a loud moan from somewhere beneath his feet. Could there be dungeons under the castle floor? If so, who or what was down there?

Remember to use your best handwriting when you want to present neat, careful work.

UNIT 8

Practising paragraphs.

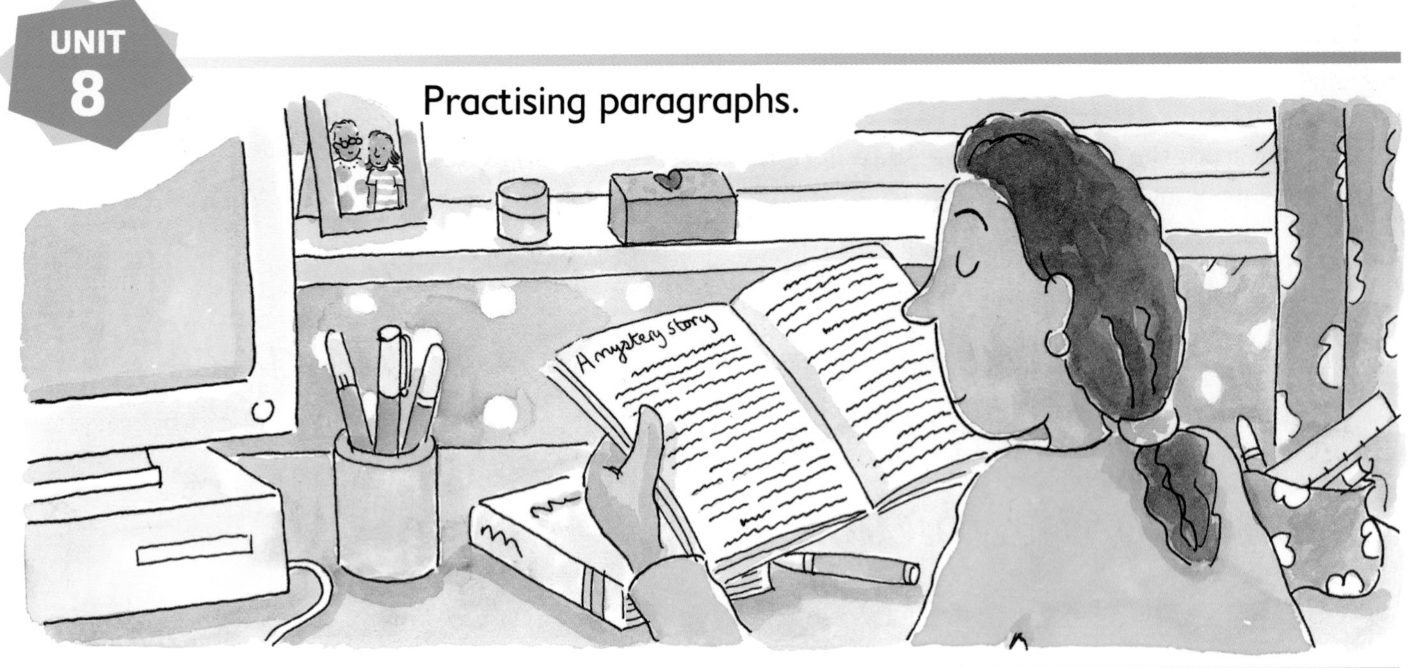

Paragraphs help you to organise your writing.

FOCUS

Copy this paragraph into your book in your best handwriting.

The Loch Ness Monster is believed to live in a loch, or lake, in Scotland. Some people claim they have seen it. Some have even taken photographs of a strange dark shape.

Remember to indent the first word of each paragraph.

XTRA

Write the sentences below into your book. Divide the sentences into two paragraphs. Remember to start each new paragraph on a new line and indent the first word.

The Abominable Snowman, or the Yeti, is said to be a huge, hairy, human-like creature living in the Himalayas. In 1957, an explorer set out on a Yeti hunt after five local people had been killed. But he didn't find the Yeti.

XTENSION

Write the sentences below into your book. Divide the sentences into three paragraphs.

In 1951, a climber took photographs of huge footprints in the snow. Could these have been made by the Yeti? An expert on snow explained that footprints made by a smaller animal could have started to melt in the midday sun and frozen again at night. Each time this happened, the footprints would have got bigger until they looked enormous. High in the mountains, the air is very thin. The lack of oxygen can make people imagine strange things.

Practising keeping letters in correct proportion.

Form your letters neatly and consistently.

A These prefixes make a word have the opposite meaning. Copy them into your book.

un de dis anti il

B Add the prefix *un* to the words below. Write the words into your book. The first one is done to help you.

un + happy = unhappy

kind
educated
helpful
identified
familiar

When you join the letter *f* to *a*, *u*, or *i*, the horizontal joining line helps you form the next letter in the correct proportion, like this:
fa fu fi

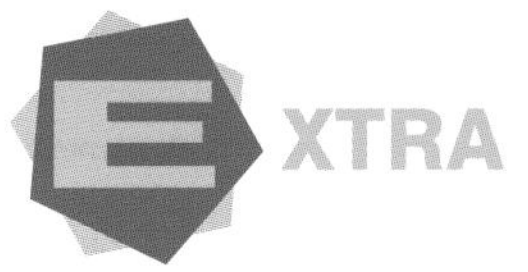

XTRA

Copy this passage into your book. Choose the correct word.

A big mystery that has so far remained solved/unsolved is this: what are the identified/unidentified flying objects that have been seen in the sky? Some people have said that they are usual/unusual cloud formations. Ufologists usually/unusually claim that the Earth is being watched by alien intelligences. If so, what do these aliens want? Will we ever discover the truth?

XTENSION

Copy this poem on to plain paper. Keep your letters in the correct proportion.

Remember, capital letters are as tall as ascenders.

UNIDENTIFIED FLYING OBJECT

There
in the night sky
with lights flashing
it swoops from high to low –
and straight away it's identified
as an unfamiliar
UFO!

By *Ronald Kay*

UNIT 10

Practising presentation.

Come to my party!

FOCUS

Practise drawing different borders on a piece of paper. You can use borders when you want to present a piece of writing attractively.

XTRA

Practise writing this text on to plain paper.

You are invited to my

ALIENS

fancy dress birthday party

on Saturday June 15th at 4 pm

at 29 The Spinneys, Chipping Aston.

From Stuart Stevens

R.S.V.P.

Draw some guidelines in pencil on your paper. This will help you keep your letters the correct height and size and your writing straight across the paper.

XTENSION

Use these instructions to design and make an invitation to 'An aliens fancy dress party' on a piece of plain paper. Don't forget to say who the invitation is for, what it is to, the day, the time, where it will take place, and who it is from.

1. Plan where your writing will go.
2. Pencil in the borders and colour them.
3. Lightly pencil in some guidelines. Use a ruler to make sure the lines are the same width apart.
4. Write in your text.
5. Rub out the pencil lines.

You are less likely to smudge your work if you start at the top left-hand corner.

This was written with a fine pen nib.

This was written with a medium pen nib.

This was written with a broad pen nib.

UNIT 11

Practising writing instructions.

Cross the road safely!

OCUS

Copy these connective words into your book.

so	but	however
also	because	furthermore
or	before	otherwise
and	therefore	as well as

Remember, the letter *f* is a tall letter and its tail falls below the line.

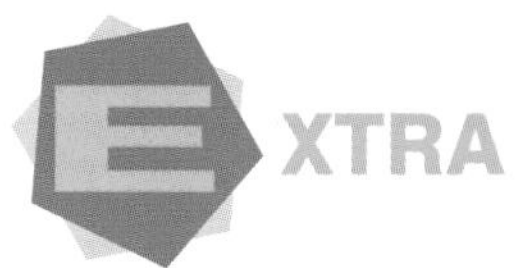

XTRA

Bullet points are often used to separate instructions. Copy these sentences into your book. Choose the correct connective word.

Take care!
You must leave the same space between the bullet point and the first letter in each sentence.

- Use a pedestrian crossing, otherwise/because choose a place where you can see in all directions.
- Always listen, otherwise/because sometimes you can hear traffic before you see it.

XTENSION

Put these instructions from The Green Cross Code into the correct order and number them. Copy the instructions into your book in your best handwriting.

Stop just before you get to the kerb.
First find a safe place to cross.
If traffic is coming, let it pass.
Look all around for traffic and listen.
When it is safe, go straight across the road - do not run.

UNIT 12

Practising writing instructions.

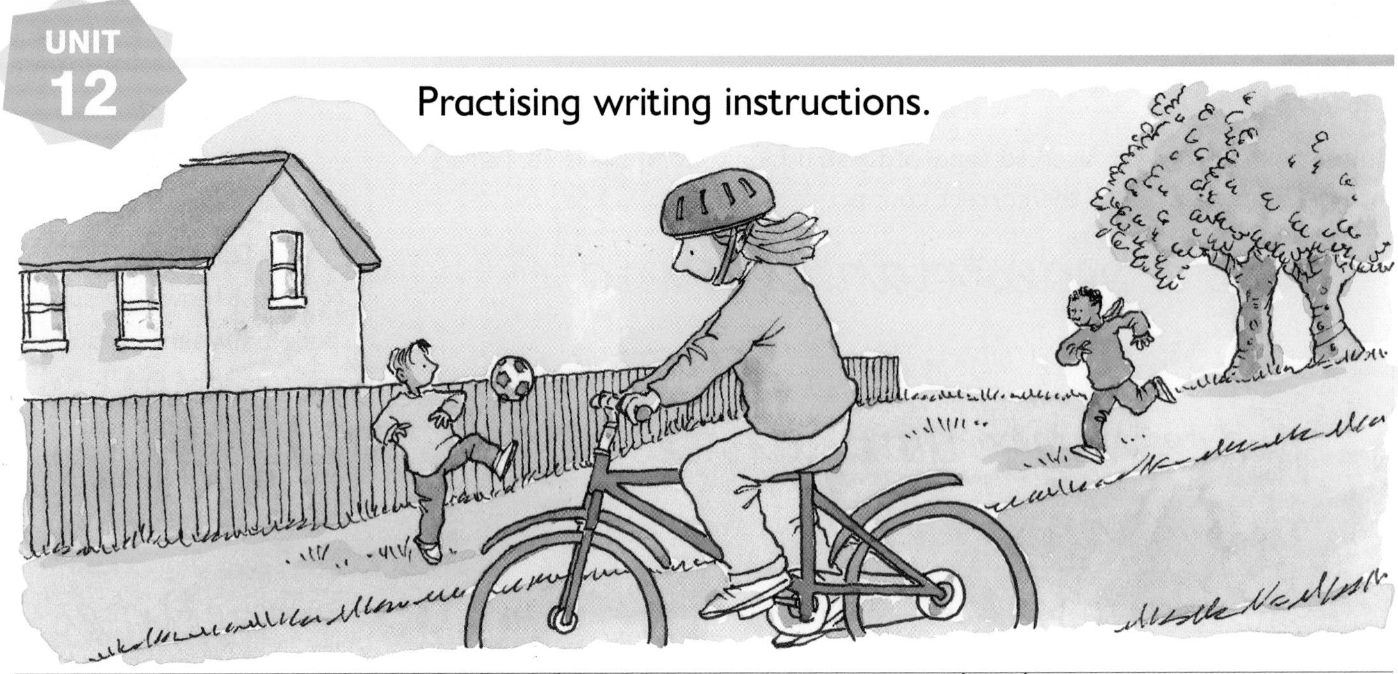

Cyclists should always wear a helmet.

OCUS

A Copy these instructions into your book.

Check! Wait! Stop! Dismount!
Choose! Watch! Steer! Disappear!

B Think of four more instruction words. Write them into your book.

XTRA

These instructions are for cyclists wanting to turn right. Copy them into your book. Add bullet points.

Remember to space out your instructions to make them clear.

Check the traffic, signal, and move to the centre of the road.
Wait until there is a safe gap in the traffic before turning.
Stop and wait on the left until there is a safe gap in the traffic.
Dismount and push your bicycle across the road.

XTENSION

Design and make a leaflet called 'Buying a bicycle'. Plan your pages. Decide where your writing will go. Will you use print writing or sloped and joined writing?

Write down the title of the leaflet. You need to include this advice for buyers:

- Check the cycle is the right size for you.
- Check the saddle and handlebars are the right height.
- Check the lights and reflectors are working properly.
- Check the brakes and gears are working efficiently.
- Check the tyres are inflated to the right pressure.

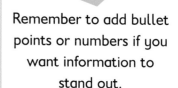

Remember to add bullet points or numbers if you want information to stand out.

UNIT 13

Practising presenting a project.

The Olympic Games – then and now.

Focus

Copy these headings into your book.

The First Olympic Games
The Olympic Ideal Today

XTRA

A Read this information.

> No one knows exactly when the Olympic Games began although official records date back to 776 BC. The Games took place every four years in the city of Olympia. They were held in honour of the god Zeus. At first there was only running but later wrestling, boxing, chariot racing, horse racing and the pentathlon were added. A winning athlete had a garland placed on his head.

B Make notes about what you have read. Write them into your book. The first one is done to help you.

First recorded games 776 BC.

Make sure your notes are legible so you can read them later.

XTENSION

A Read these notes.

Remember to use your best handwriting for finished work.

> Modern Olympics symbolise friendly international competition
>
> Take place every four years
>
> Honour individual endeavour
>
> Gold, silver and bronze medals awarded instead of garlands
>
> First Winter Olympics Chamonix 1924

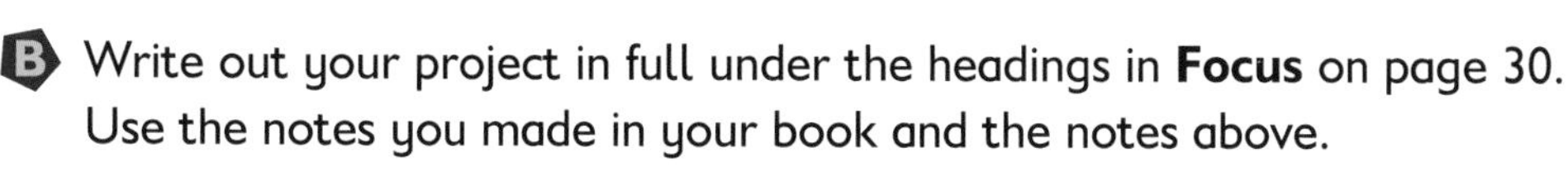

B Write out your project in full under the headings in **Focus** on page 30. Use the notes you made in your book and the notes above.

C Illustrate your project with pictures of Olympic events.

UNIT 14

Practising fluency.

Narcissus loved to admire himself.

FOCUS

Copy these pronouns into your book.

he	you	we	them	I
her	your	me	they	it
him	yours	she	their	us

Remember, joining your letters helps you to write quickly and fluently.

XTRA

Copy this passage into your book. Use the pronouns *him* or *he* instead of 'Narcissus' sometimes to make the passage easier to read.

Narcissus was very handsome. Many people came to Narcissus and said they loved Narcissus but Narcissus treated them all the same. Narcissus rejected them.

Sloping your writing will help you develop fluency.

XTENSION

Copy this passage into your book. Make sure your writing is fluent, joined and legible.

Narcissus thought he was beautiful. He wanted to share his life with someone equally beautiful.

One day, as he was walking in the forest, he felt he was being followed. "Show yourself!" he shouted. "Show yourself," a voice replied. The words were the same, but the voice was so beautiful. "Let me see you," he pleaded. "Let me see you," the voice replied.

A nymph called Echo appeared. But Narcissus rejected her when he realised that all she could do was repeat what had just been said.

UNIT 15

Practising writing double letters.

Fossils were hidden in the cliffs.

FOCUS

A Copy these double letters into your book. Make sure both letters are the same height and size.

cc oo ee rr ff ss ll tt mm

When you have finished writing a letter, take your pen back up to the top ready to write the next letter. Remember, all letters start at the top, except *d* and *e*.

B These words contain double letters. Copy the words into your book.

cliff possible illegal mammal
stiff fossil illiterate mammoth
tiff missile illegible mummy

XTRA

Choose the correct word to finish these sentences. Copy the sentences into your book.

1 The children found a fossil/fossils at the bottom of the cliffs.

2 The man was cross and tosses/tossed the treasure into the sea.

3 The lorry carry/carried stone away from Cliffside Quarry.

XTENSION

Copy this passage into your book.

When writing *ff*, begin the first letter at the top and make sure the tail goes below the line. Join the next letter from the cross of the first *f*.

With its steep cliffs and hidden coves, the Isle of Wight was once a smugglers' haunt. In some places, the cliffs are over a hundred metres tall.

In the 1920s, an area called Undercliff was battered by a succession of storms and slipped into the sea. New treasures were revealed, including the fossil of an iguanodon and the fossilised remains of many other dinosaurs.

UNIT 16

Practising speedwriting.

Quick! Write this down!

FOCUS

When speedwriting, it can be quicker to use a shorter word in place of the original word. These words are different ways of saying 'dig', 'buried' and 'box'. Copy them into your book as fast as you can.

(dig)	excavate	tunnel	investigate	probe
(buried)	entombed	hidden	immersed	covered
(box)	case	trunk	container	chest

EXTRA

These are quickly written notes about the location of some treasure. Write the directions out in full into your book. Make sure your handwriting is neat.

Wlk 6 stps nth of lghthse.
Tke 10 stps est.
Go cave.
Fllow undgrd tnnl.
X mrks spot.

EXTENSION

Copy these sentences into your book in speedwriting.

1 There is a steep cliff around the cove.
2 The treasure chest is under the rock.
3 There are gold coins in the box.
4 The pirates land on the beach.
5 They excavate beneath the rock.
6 They find the treasure and carry it up the cliff.

Use the shortened forms of words (*there's*) and some different, shorter words (*box*, *dig*) if you think it will help you to write quickly.

UNIT 17

Ensuring letters are in the correct proportion.

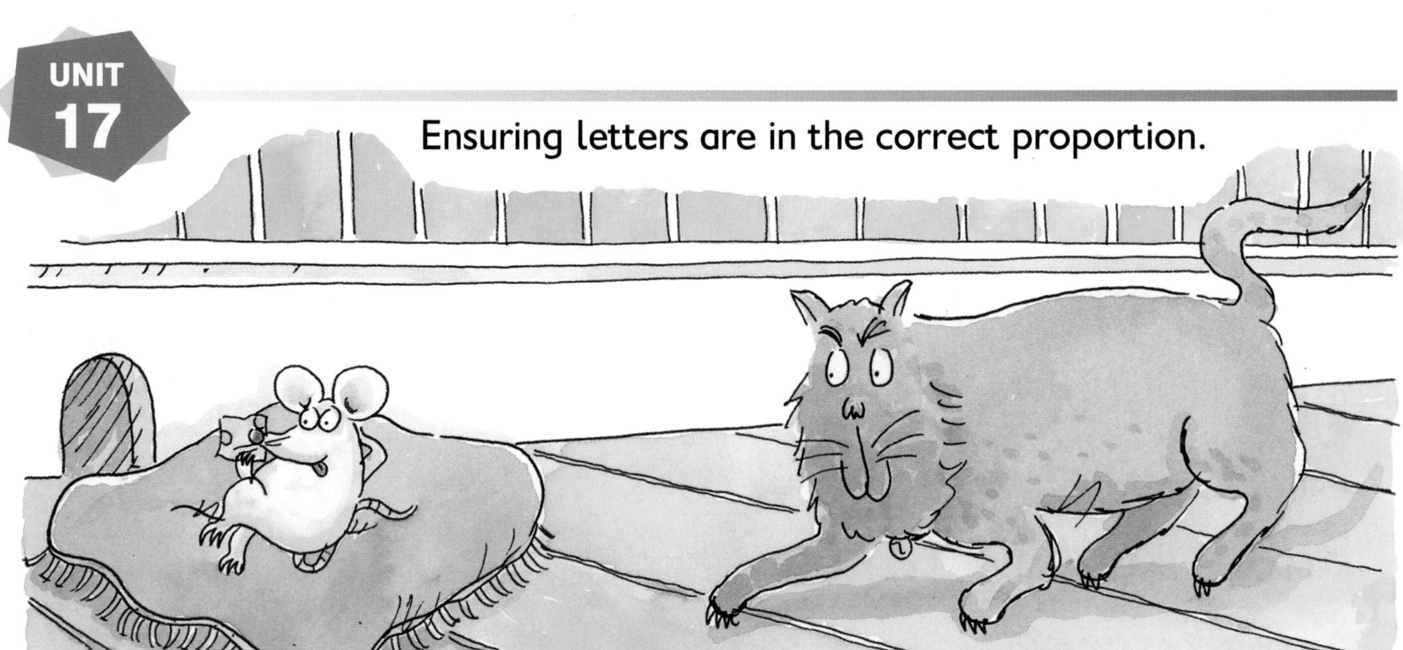

The cat was as quiet as a mouse.

FOCUS

Copy these similes into your book.

as quiet as a mouse
as hungry as a wolf
as fresh as a daisy
as brave as a lion

Remember, a descender, or tail, on a letter always falls below the line, like this:

f g j p q y

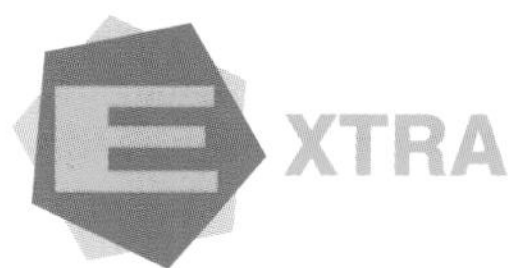

EXTRA

Choose the correct word to finish these similes. Copy the similes into your book.

as steady as a... book/rock/jelly

as slow as a... hare/mouse/tortoise

as cold as... ice/custard/pasta

as green as... milk/a horse/grass

EXTENSION

Think of a simile to finish each sentence. Copy the sentences into your book.
Make sure your letters are in the correct proportion to each other.

> Remember,
> the letter *t* is not as tall as other letters with an ascender.

1 The cat was as quick as ______.

2 The dog was as cool as a ______ as the cat leapt towards him.

3 The cat's eyes sparkled like ______.

4 Mrs Smith's hat was as flat as a ______ after Tom sat on it!

UNIT 18

Practising presentation.

Copy this poem into your book. Make it look as attractive as you can.

Remember, it is easier to slope your letters to the right if you turn your paper at a slight angle and pull the pen strokes in the correct direction.

MARMALADE

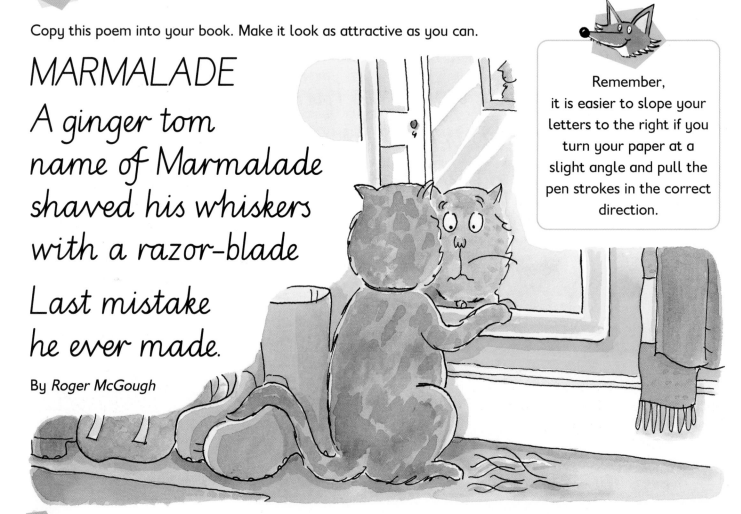

A ginger tom
name of Marmalade
shaved his whiskers
with a razor-blade

Last mistake
he ever made.

By *Roger McGough*

XTRA

A kenning is a way of describing something without saying what it is. This poem is a list of kennings. Copy it into your book.

A toe-nibbler
A dark-dreamer
A paw-padder
A floor-scratcher
A warm-sleeper
A night-creeper
A fur-cleaner
A flea-finder
A mouse-hunter
A house-minder
A secret-hoarder
A china-breaker
A four-foot-lander

'Cat' by *Rachel Myers*

Think about presentation. Plan where your poem will begin and end. Will you start your poem at the side of the page, or will you write it in the middle?

XTENSION

Write your own poem about a kitten using kennings. Start by making some quick notes. Then write a first draft into your book. Use your best handwriting for the final copy.

Remember to add a border to decorate your poem.

Practising printing.

Print letters are easy to read.

FOCUS

A Copy the print alphabet into your book.

Aa Bb Cc Dd Ee Ff Gg Hh Ii Jj Kk Ll Mm
Nn Oo Pp Qq Rr Ss Tt Uu Vv Ww Xx Yy Zz

B These words use lower-case print letters. Copy the words into your book.

run	swim	snorkel	dig
running	swimming	snorkelling	digging
runner	swimmer	snorkeller	digger

Carefully written print is good for adverts and posters because it stands out.

EXTRA

Copy this advert on to plain paper. Use the print alphabet.

DREAMLAND EUROPE

So much to see and do:

- swim
- snorkel
- dig for gold
- run The Dreamland Challenge

EXTENSION

Copy this poster on to a sheet of plain paper. Fill in the activities section.
Make sure you use the print alphabet.

STEP INTO A WORLD OF MAGIC

Come to

DREAMLAND EUROPE

So many activities to enjoy:

21, rue Bougainvillaea

12345 Marseille, France

Remember to draw pencil lines on your paper to help you make the letters the correct size and height.

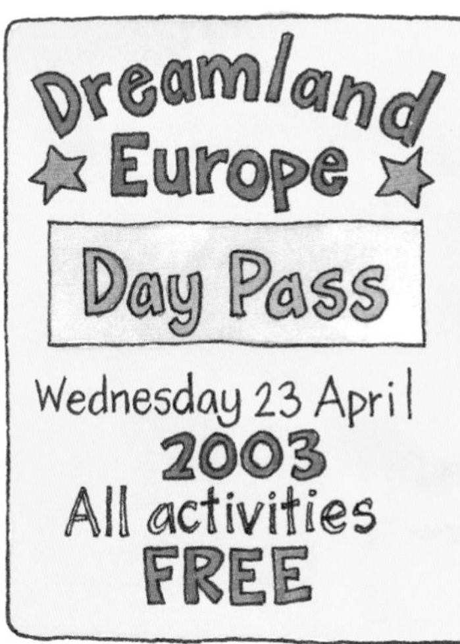

Dreamland
Europe
Day Pass
Wednesday 23 April
2003
All activities
FREE

UNIT 20

Developing an individual handwriting style.

loopy writing round writing
jagged writing pointy writing

FOCUS

Everyone develops different styles of handwriting. Some people make joins after the letters *b* and *p*. Other people add loops from the letters *f*, *g*, *j* and *y*. Write these words into your book. Try joining all your letters except capitals.

Tokyo Beijing Uruguay South Africa
Seychelles Majorca Paraguay Tenerife
Malaysia Fiji Egypt California

XTRA

Remember, even in an individual style of writing you must form your letters consistently.

These sentences are in different writing styles. Copy them into your book.

1 Tokyo was the most crowded place I visited on my travels.

2 Every morning the famous Bullet Train brought passengers into the city.

3 I saw amazing buildings, including an office block only two metres wide.

4 Each morning I joined hundreds of people exercising in the park.

XTENSION

Copy this extract into your book. Remember to use your own preferred style of writing.

Hachiko was the pet dog of a professor at Tokyo University who used to meet his master off the train as he returned from work each day. After his master died while at work, Hachiko still turned up at the same spot, every day, for the next seven years. In admiration of this display of loyalty, the people of Tokyo had a statue built at the place where he waited.

From ***'Full Circle'*** by *Michael Palin*

CHECK-UP

You should now be able to join your letters using the four joins.
Copy these words into your book.

him her and so dinner digging
biped bicycle happy unhappy because

illegible illegal transport transplant
snorkelling unfamiliar California Tenerife

counteract countermove lorries crosses
before therefore furthermore box

whined whistled counterfeit counterfoil
otherwise parasol cliffs bipartite

EXTRA

You should now be able to write quickly, neatly and legibly.

A Copy these words into your book.

investigate
identified
otherwise
furthermore

B Write the word *investigate* as many times as you can in 30 seconds.

C This sentence contains all the joins. Copy it into your book in your best handwriting.

The police began to investigate why the box was buried near the cliffs.

D Practise writing the sentence above quickly, neatly and legibly.
Time yourself to find out how quickly you can write the sentence.

XTENSION

Copy this poem on to plain paper. Use guidelines underneath. Set the poem out carefully and neatly, remembering all you have learnt about presenting your work.

Marbles in my pocket,
Blue and green and red,
And some are yellow-golden,
And some are brown instead.

Marbles in the playground,
Big and little ring –
Oh, I like playing marbles,
But that's a different thing.

Marbles in my pocket,
Smooth within my hand,
That's the part that's nicest;
Do you understand?

Marbles in my pocket
To rattle when I run!
For winter days are here again,
And marble-time's begun!

From ***'Marbles in my Pocket'*** by *Lydia Pender*